# TRANSITIONING

# Transitioning

TWILIGHT NEWCOMB

Charleston, SC
www.PalmettoPublishing.com

*Transitioning*
Copyright © 2023 by Twilight Newcomb

All rights reserved
No portion of this book may be reproduced, stored in a retrieval system, or transmitted in any form by any means–electronic, mechanical, photocopy, recording, or other–except for brief quotations in printed reviews, without prior permission of the author.

First Edition

Paperback ISBN: 979-8-8229-0496-5

*Every transition is different  
This is my transition*

# Twilight

I knew I was Twilight one morning.
I woke up
And I said,
"I'm Twilight."
This happens to us.
We have a dead name.
It's the name everyone knew us by,
And then another name claims us.
We ask who we are.
"Who am I?"
We're like a baby,
A female baby who's born.
And so, one morning,
Early,
I was Twilight,
And there weren't any other names.
And now Twilight talks to herself
And says,
"What are you going to do about that Twilight?"
"What do you think about that?"
And it's becoming more and more natural.
I never think about
The old one before.
His name never comes up.
He is gone
And he can't come back.
Twilight's here

# What I see women do

Now I'm allowed to be among them.
I don't talk
Much.
I just sit there,
Listen,
And what I see them do
Is bring love
To keep everything from falling apart.
The men won't do it.
Maybe some,
But the women do it all the time,
Bringing love.
Someone's mother dies
And that baby goes to another mother,
And that mother is the sister of the mother that died,
Or a neighbor,
Or the baby may come
For the first time to her doorstep,
And the new mother knows
She will take all the heartache,
Will take all the tears,
The bloody knees,
Every car crash,
Maybe an open box,
And she doesn't say a word.

And when she takes this new baby,
Her baby,
The other women
Don't even blink.
They don't look up.
In the group, when it is said,
This love sacrifice,
This bringing of the love,
With everything it means,
Is just something women do.
And the boys
Are hopeless.
Are they going to give up everything
To help someone
They may not know?
I wish boys had to live a year as a woman,
Just to see how lucky they are.

# Women have love

They have love a lot of the time.
I like to be around them.
When I am around them,
Maybe I don't see them really,
But you see,
I feel peace.
I feel kindness.
I feel acceptance.
We sit together.
Everybody gets a chance.
Nobody has to put somebody down.
Nobody has to be top dog.
And it's us,
And we are together.
When our meeting is over,
We break into small groups,
Two or three,
Often two,
Just laughing
And smiling at each other.
And if someone is sad, there are lots of hugs
And sometimes tears.
It really is different
Being a girl and not a guy.
If more men
Lived the way I have lived,
They would be with us.

# Welcoming in

It's so lovely
To watch people
Who have been completely alone,
Who have been in a dark room for a month,
Who come out once,
Who never speak,
And then there are two
Like crippled birds.
They hop toward each other.
There's a group flying,
And suddenly they're not crippled anymore
And they take flight,
And I watch them in the sky,
Flying with all the other beautiful birds.
They came from darkness,
And now the light is on their wings,
And it's a galaxy of birds above me
Wheeling in the sky.

# A man will

Cut your heart in two
Until you have a dead heart,
And put the pieces back inside you
Where they will never beat again,
Where you will not be able to love again,
Where you will be dead inside.
A man will
Use your body
And watch you love it,
And throw your heart
In a dumpster
Like dirty clothing.
A man will explode in your life.
He will take you to tulip fields,
Put flowers in your hair
And detonate
And leave a mess in the sun.
Their power
Is they do not care.
They are like an alien
From a different planet.
They discovered a species
And watch the glistening tears,
See the pointed finger,
Feel an uncomfortable
Tugging at their heart.
They're attracted to this
Beautiful species,
And they collect them,

And they use them,
And they see the tears,
Their ruined faces,
Broken voices,
The crying in the dark.
But when you look at their face,
It is unmoving.
They feel shame and guilt,
But not enough
To leave the planet.
But they want to leave the planet.
They tire
Pulling wings off butterflies,
Of taking what is beautiful
And making it weep.
There are many men like this.
They are ashamed of what they are.
They know they are an inferior species.
They have met a better race.
But still, they walk among us
As if they come from a kind planet
Filled with love,
But they put the silencer on their heart
And murder souls
And see the dead bodies
Of these poor creatures
Who could not bear the pain.
They walk among us,
Parading as loving beings
And their many incarnations
Lead to women's graves.

# Some boys need a time out

They're slamming the life out of us.
We show them our butterflies.
They want to come inside and play with us.
We are very beautiful in the morning meadows,
Sunlight overhead,
Dancing from flower to flower,
Flapping our wings,
And they see us.
We know we're beautiful.
We know we're pretty.
We know we're everything you need.
And so, what do you do?
You want to tear our wings off.
You want to slam the life out of us.
You want to put a pretty butterfly on your shelf
And tell it when to fly,
Tell it when to stop on that flower that you're pointing at.
These boys need a time out.
A long time out.
We butterflies are getting together.
It's a fact you have to hide.
You do your tearing a butterfly's wings off
Behind closed doors.

You're careful about raising your voice.
You never put anything in writing.
And you say,
"Stop lying about me.
I'm not tearing your wings off."
And some of us are lying on the floor,
And we're dead.

# The trapdoor inside women

Men look for the trapdoor inside women.
They don't even know they have it,
But when the man finds it,
He comes in through the trapdoor,
And the woman hates herself.
She finds out she has a trapdoor,
That she can be used
As if she is nothing.
Men share information
About where girls' trapdoors are.
This is pretty horrible,
But they conspire together.
They share secrets.
They show other men where the woman's trapdoor is.
They laugh about a woman in love
Who thinks he loves her,
Who's only using her.
They like to see her swept away by her
Love,
By her emotions, her feelings,
His touch upon her breasts.
Watch the current of her heart
Flowing against
The coastline of his body,
Of what they are,
And they feel the gentle lapping of her love
As it inhabits every nook and cranny,
The soft eddies of her spirit against him.
They look at each other from the sides of their eyes.

They are lost in laughing.
They chuckle about it.
They shake their heads
And glance up at each other.
A man can tell when a woman's Spirit has fallen through the trapdoor.
They are broken.
Now he can do whatever he wants.
The men observe it.
The women observe it also.
I don't know what they think.
I think they feel sorry for a girl
Who finds out she has a trapdoor
And doesn't know it,
And feels her spirit dropping through it
Suddenly.
It is like a place where they hang people,
A gallows,
And men watch women,
Looking for their trapdoors.
Once a woman has gone through her trapdoor
And somehow pulled herself back
Onto the surface of the gallows,
Maybe her leg is hanging down into darkness.
She knows it's there.
She can't forget.
She realizes something about men:
Men want to use her body,
When they want to use her body
And they don't care about her.
They want to use her in every way.
They are ready to trade her
For a cuter girl,
A prettier girl,

A sweeter girl,
And when they finish,
Women are watchful.
They know what can happen
When a pure heart
Has the life squeezed from it.
Now they are a girl with a trapdoor,
And they have to guard their trapdoor against men,
Because they know some men are looking
And want to be inside them,
And own them,
And hold her heart in their hands
And watch it beating,
Turn her into a warm-blooded
Pink cadaver,
Waiting for their touch
And guidance.

# In over my head

Sometimes I'm in over my head.
I can look up, and the waters are closing above me.
I have to keep my mouth closed
As I sink down and down.
Sometimes you have to run out of there.
You just have to get all your stuff,
What you can grab.
You just catch glimpses of what's important
And grab it and throw it in a bag,
And you're trying not to panic,
And you know you're leaving everything behind.
Run back in,
Quietly not making any noise,
Not shutting any doors,
Being completely quiet,
Taking a little bit of your life
That's gone forever
And walking out the door
And closing it quietly behind you.

# The boys have to go so the sisters can live

Boys, your day is done.
We can't have you
Spoiling all our fun.
You can't be black clouds
Across our sun.
For too long
You have dragged us into a valley of darkness.
We don't deserve to be in your valley of darkness.
I know it's your valley,
But we are leaving.
We have already left.
I know you are a crying child.
I know you want your mommy,
And you use that when you're ready,
When you think the love trap
That we will never get out of
Is prepared.
You're hunting the heart of a girl
Who never did you any harm.
So, my sisters are going to go free.
Your day is over.
Sit there and think
How this happened.
The ache in your heart
Is yours now
And we are free.

# The estradiol patch the progesterone

The man actually disappears.
A girl appears.
You have your old face,
But you soften.
You bring someone else.
Your pores get small.
You were balding;
Your hair grows back.
It's thick,
Not 71.
Your eyes change colors.
I was hazel,
Now I'm blue.
My voice is a girl's voice.
It's the only one I use.
When I talk like a man,
I keep gagging.
So, there's a girl looking at you,
And you're gallant,
And sometimes I can tell you're interested.
That's only the beginning,
Because now I dream girls' dreams.

But sometimes, I look in the mirror.
The hormones aren't working.
I see a man.
It's just not right.
So, I need to talk to the doctor,
Be who I am becoming.

# The water is coming

More and more,
I can feel the female waters
Flowing over the male continent.
I find myself crying.
It's soft and not violent.
It just happens.
Tears.
I say something
And express my appreciation
Of the love of others,
Both men and women,
And I break down.
The twigs holding my voice
Weaken, fall apart;
I tumble in on myself
And trail off.
It is like a shallow shoreline
Within me,
With water lapping softly,
Rising on the shore.
Soon the female ocean
Will cover everything.
The continent will be buried below
And never seen again.
The waters will move with the moon,
And the continent
Will be still
Beneath the waves.

# Today I saw a girl at the intersection

She was African American.
She was wearing a jumpsuit.
And she walked across
In front of me,
And her hands were saying,
"I'm a lost girl.
Somebody help me."
And her hands were opening and closing.
They were held down in front of her,
Like they were saying,
"Something's happened."
Something she did not understand,
Something she didn't have words for,
And her hands were opening and closing
Like something had fallen out of them,
Like she was saying,
"Look what's happened
To me."
But there was no me.
There were only the hands opening and closing.
They communicated a great loss.
She was perpetually
Walking around,
Feeling a loss.
Her hands were whimpering.

Her face was blank with grief.
Her soul had collapsed
Into tearless weeping,
And that was all she could feel.
Nothing else.
I felt so sorry for her.
She was young,
She was attractive,
But I didn't feel any lust.
I just felt so sorry.
She was alone.
She had lost her mind.
She was like a child.
Then she started across the street
In the direction I was driving,
And her hands were opening and closing.
They were saying, "I'm lost.
I'm afraid.
Please, somebody, help me."
She was not an adult walking through
An early Tucson morning.
If she had been the size of a child,
People would have stopped their cars.
They would have gotten out and helped her.
They wouldn't allow a child to wander around like that in traffic.
She had the mind of a child.
At 6:40 in the morning,
A girl was lost at an intersection.
She was frightened and alone.
It is sad to see a girl
Crying with her hands
And no one helps her,

But I don't know what I could have done.
She was not
Of right mind.
She was speaking with her lost face.
She was speaking with her hands,
And she was walking away.
She was a child
In an adult's body
Wandering through Tucson
By herself.

## Only three years ago

I was with them as a man
And now I am invisible.
They don't know who I am.
I don't wear makeup,
My voice is a girl's voice,
I wear a dress,
I weigh 300 pounds,
And they just sleepwalk through me.
So, I watch them.
I can visit
In a different dimension.
Before, one was on my left,
One was on my right.
Now I am talking to them by themselves.
They smile at me.
The girls smile at me.
The boys smile at me.
I tell them my name is Twilight.
Later, after an hour,
I tell them my dead name.
We drank coffee together.
We were chummy.
Now:
"No, I don't remember you."
And they're looking right at me
With a blank, kind face.

# GRS

What you don't know:
The most important change
Is in your head.
There's a woman in there,
And with the estradiol,
The progesterone,
The girl is dreaming in you,
Dreaming of the things girls dream about:
Guys.
They are in their dreams now.
They are in your dreams now.
It's not just something that hangs from you,
Something that moves in the wind slightly,
Something that knows you're in the room.
A guy, a girl.
When you go that far,
You are saying goodbye to the man in your heart.
You are saying goodbye to the man in your mind.
You are saying goodbye to the man in your soul.
That man is going to die,
Because there will be a woman,
And I guess I will learn who she is.

# Goodbye blaine

I remember you,
And you're really going to be gone.
I can remember you now,
Because you're in me.
You're like a thin skeleton.
Remember everything you've done
But soon, the skeleton will be released.
It won't matter anymore.
You will be like a morning mist
Rising
And the new sun will come,
And you will disappear.
I won't be able to remember you anymore
As blaine.
I'll be an amnesiac
Trying to remember what it felt like to be a man.
I'll be on the other side
In the pool of water;
You'll be below the surface.
I'll be able to see you,
Able to remember you, but when I reach down to touch you,
The water will ripple.
Won't be able to see your face.
You'll sink deeper below the surface.

I really won't be a man anymore;
I'll be a woman looking at a man
Below the surface of the water
I can never dive into.
You will be gone forever.
I will watch you sink deeper and deeper
Into the water,
Until you are white.
And then I will see black water,
And you will be gone.

# On the other side

I'm hopeful.
The operation was three days ago.
I will never have a man's eyes again.
I know it is hard to believe,
But the eyes have changed color.
They're blue now.
They used to be hazel.
There's no testosterone, so they lighten.
They are a gentle woman's eyes.
Other women tell me this.
I look in the mirror
And a man does not look back at me.
There is no one to meet you
At the property line,
No one to go chest to chest.
He is gone,
No one that needs to be the center of attention.
She can watch from the corner,
And watch boys
Vying for approval,
And be glad she's not a man.
And I'm shrinking;
I've lost an inch.
Usually, we lose an inch to two and a half inches.
Then the strength goes;
The arms shed their muscle.

I will be weak.
But the anger is gone.
I'm not melancholy.
I'm not morose.
I'm serene.
Already the dreams are becoming more emotional,
And I'm getting more concerned,
Waking up a little anxious.
I've never had emotional dreams.
I've always been indifferent.
But now the emotions are growing.
Women spend lots of time worrying.
I see how much I've hurt the women in my life.
It was hard being a man and knowing I was hurting them.
A man being a man
Cares about the path he takes every day,
And it's very important to him,
And even if it's not important,
He thinks it is.
He's making fateful decisions
With consequences that matter.
But most of what he does
Is inconsequential.
But no one tells him
That he's like all the others,
Because that would hurt his feelings.
They shelter their child
From knowing
That he is just another salesman,
Just another caretaker.
They make him feel special.

So, as he goes humming on his way,
He doesn't know he's a foolish little man.
They do this because they love him.
And he makes mistakes,
And does not tower,
And in all his frailty,
The women help him believe in himself,
In all his weakness,
That he is special,
And that is because
He is special to them.

# Things are better now

Looking back at my poetry,
I was miserable.
I was in the middle
Of my parents' death,
Of failing in many ways,
And I didn't have much hope.
When the opportunity came,
I measured the alley
From the back door of the bar
To my house,
And was happy.
But that has ended.
I don't want to drown myself anymore.
I have hope.
There I was staggering against the stars,
Just hanging on,
Ashamed and guilty I couldn't do better,
Didn't do better.
But now I'm at peace.
I don't hide sharp objects.
I don't cover up my mirrors.
And amazingly,
I'm a different sex.
I'm just quiet now,
Getting ready
For a peaceful time.

Finally, maybe,
At peace with myself
After so many years
Of running.
The desperate accumulation
Of redeeming qualities
Couldn't stop me
From yelling "I hate myself"
When I looked in the mirror,
Never feeling I was enough.
Now I'm living
in a peaceful world,
And hopefully able
To bring peace to others.

# I am beginning to see

Love all around me.
When I sit in a room
And I pay attention,
I remember
That the life
We save
Is our own
When we help others.
This is so different.
And the way I've lived,
Why would I take the time
To help someone
So far gone?
But if I'm in God's hands,
There is no measure
Which I can use.
I already have enough.
I have everything I need.
If I'm helping others,
They are worthy because they need my help,
And they are helping me the same way.
Everything I did before
Was because I felt less than.
I was so busy filling that hole
That I didn't have time for others.
They were just a means
To make me feel better
About myself.

But now, if I'm in God's hands,
I am enough.
Helping people in front of me
Not selfishly,
Not dishonestly,
Not fearfully,
Not resentfully.
When I look around the room,
I see people hugging each other.
I see people patting each other,
Holding hands,
Smiling at each other,
And never have I seen
So much love.
Now that I am looking for God's love,
I see it all around me.
It was always there.
But now my eyes are opening.
The days are becoming more beautiful.
Seeing God's love gives me hope.
I have ups and downs,
But if I look,
I see God carrying many people.
We are being held.
We are protected.
I can see the love that binds us together,
And when I talk to them,
They give me more love than I expect.
They are giving and receiving all around me.
All I have to do
Is look around
And listen.

# Someone said

We need to meditate.
You need to be still.
Meditation
Opens the door.
We can be guided.
What is the voice of God?
Is it a whisper?
Is it a wind through the woods?
Is it the sound of leaves rustling
Above my head?
In a park alone,
Looking up at the dark clouds,
Thunderstorms above,
Is God talking to me then?
I know I see God
When I see people smiling at each other.
I know I see God
When I see two people with tears in their eyes
Reaching out and hugging.
I know I see God
When someone stands up from their chair
And carries tissues
To someone weeping.

I see God
When people pick their dog up
And hug it.
I see God
When women go into the other room
To check on their children playing.
God is all around me.
Now I can see.

# I am a witness

I have seen.
I report the love
God freely gives
To all of us.
You are a witness also,
And you have seen.
You have reached out your hand.
You have reassured,
Whether gruffly,
Like a man giving,
Groaning up,
But giving,
Impelled to give,
Leaning on his sword to give.
You have given love,
And women also,
In their own way.
You are a witness to who you are.
You were made to love,
And this is what matters most.
When you look at the mirror,
Your past is a web over your face,
But beyond that,
There are times that you speak your love,

And it is heard by another person,
And when they look at you,
The face they see
Has no web;
It is only a shining face,
Bringing them
Out of darkness
Into the light.

# God's love heals

Sit in a room.
Look around.
You will see love
All around you.
Look to your left,
And someone is smiling at someone.
Someone is getting out of their seat
To greet someone.
You can see God's love if you look,
But if you're not looking for it,
If you are only seeing darkness,
Then you will see darkness.
But you have this choice:
Look upon darkness all day long
And your life will become dark,
And it will become darker and darker,
And you may become a demon on the earth;
But look up to God's love,
Reach out and hold someone else's hand
When you see them crying,
Pat their shoulder,
Rest their hands in yours.
Your fingers intertwine.

You guard them on either side,
Your hand in theirs,
And your friend's hands in theirs,
And you will see their head
Moving up in thanks.
Then you are doing God's will.
It is simple.
Open to God's love all around you,
And you can heal
And be healed.

# When you have pain

Bring God's love to it.
Sometimes there are things
That are eating you alive,
And you are trembling in it,
But if you say it to another person,
Someone you can trust,
You can see God's love in their eyes.
And then they're hurting,
And the love in their eyes
Is a bridge into your soul,
Bringing you cleansing Waters.
The pain
Is covered.
You are being washed by God's love,
And you feel it.
There is relief.
Maybe you're both crying
When this happens.
You are more real
Than you were before.
You are in God's love.
You feel God's love,
And you know what's real.
You know God exists.
God is in you.
God is in them.
And your hearts speak to each other
In God's love.

# I'm enough

I'm in God's hands.
I'm enough.
I don't need to embellish.
I don't need to perform.
I don't need to lie.
I don't have to please you.
I don't have to displease you
To feel that I am more than I am.
I thank God that I am enough.
I have been given this gift
By the grace of God.
All of us.
I am carried by Him.
I do not know my future.
I do not know what will happen five minutes from now,
Or seconds from now,
But I need to remember always
That I am enough,
That I am in God's hands,
That I am in my Father's hands.

# More and more

I'm grateful for each breath.
I started my morning
Thanking God for my breath.
As I drive,
I look at the mountains,
The cars passing in the distance,
The clouds,
Shadows on the peaks.
I take a deep breath
And I hold it.
I'm very lucky I am breathing.
I'm very lucky I haven't damaged my health.
I'm very lucky I'm not in pain.
I'm very lucky I'm not sad.
I'm very lucky I'm hopeful
That I will have a breath tomorrow.
Things are getting simpler,
And I am grateful.
I start by saying thank you,
And it goes on and on,
And this is while I'm breathing,
So tomorrow maybe I'll wake up.
Maybe I'll be alive.
Every day I pray
That in the morning,
I begin by thanking God
For another day
And a chance to live.

# The little things

Life is trivial
Until it isn't,
And you know you're walking down your last road,
And no matter what happens,
You will end soon.
Won't be any new beginnings
Here on earth.
There will be time to maybe right some wrongs,
To bring closure.
Soon you will never see another sunrise.
The rain will never be upon your face again,
Never able to touch your child.
And so, all the dreams,
Things that keep us going
For more and better,
Fall away
When you meet someone who
Will soon see their last fog covered mountain,
Butterflies in the backyard,
A hug from a friend.
Then everything is trivial
In comparison.
Everything you believe
Is well enough,
But this could be you
Going down your final road,
Facing your final sunset,
Or facing your final sunrise,
And you realize

This is what matters.
You're only here for a day,
But you give, and
It's not your big dreams,
It's not what you're going to make.
You are here to heal,
Give comfort,
And fill the spaces
In the hearts of people
Who need those spaces filled.
You're capable of doing that.
So, this is a
Wonderful guide
To keep you human,
And as people are exiting
They bring the gift
Of remembering why we're here.

# Today I was in a place

Where there were only women.
This is a place where we feel free
To cry.
And as people spoke,
Stories touched us.
Pain that could not be spoken,
Only gestured at
With a head
Motion toward the past,
And things that happened,
And fighting back tears,
They continued.
They spoke of a time,
Some of them,
When God was in their life, suddenly,
Miraculously.
It was just another day,
And then something happened,
And it was a sign,
And they remember this.
They shared it today
And it's an anchor for me now.
I have been with people many times
When they describe the miraculous
Appearance of God in their life.

They got down on their knees
And they prayed,
And peace came over them,
And they were never the way they were before.
So, I'm not tired of crying,
But I cry the way girls do.
It just happens, and the tears are flowing.
It feels good to be in a space
With many women
Where we are joined together
In love.

# *I was a man*

Who is now allowed in women's spaces.
Three years ago,
I was a man all the time,
But now hours go by
And there are just women in the room,
And that is where I want to be.
If you said
There is a door;
If you go through that door,
You will be with men.
Men will be around you all the time
And will be all you see,
Men will be all you know,
But you will remember women,
I could not live there,
Remembering.
So that door is not opening.
I am allowed to be with women all the time.
I arrange my time during the day
So that I am in women's groups.
A man reading this
Will never be in this place,
And it's sad.
No one seems to notice
The men who never knew
What it is to be among women.

But that is almost all the men.
A few of us are here among you,
And the women accept me,
Treat me as one of them,
And I sit there looking at them,
Thankful
That I have come here
To be.
I live this way,
I will end this way,
Among women.

# *I am a witness*

Whenever you are alone,
Remember you are not alone.
All around you,
Near you,
Someone is reaching out with love in their heart.
Somehow you forget.
We listen only to our own voice.
You stop listening for other voices.
Somehow, we spiral down
Into the bottom of a
A deep, dark, black shaft.
Questions spin around our heads,
And they spin more and more.
Things get darker and darker,
But if we just get up
And move,
Join others,
There are many places
Where you can see people reaching out in love.
And then the dark shaft,
The black night,
The day of despair,
The night of questioning,
Becomes a memory.

All we have to remember
Is to seek the love of others,
And do not spiral into
A world,
A false world,
Where we believe we are all alone.

# Yesterday

A bright yellow tree,
A miracle,
With sun shining through;
Looking up at it,
Taking the space between
Two white buildings,
To see the sun through the leaves,
But protecting my eyes.
In a brilliant yellow
With hints of brown,
And then the white bench
I stood beside.
Sat down and looked,
The yellow canopy,
The warm sun on my face:
Beautiful.
In these last days of fall,
In summer heat
Still in the sun,
And winter is days away.
Thank you for the yellow tree
On this fall day
At the beginning of winter.

# The yellow tree's

Leaves are gone.
Splendid, brilliant yellow,
Now just bare branches;
Days before
Filling the sky,
And now empty
With no leaves at all.
They are all gone,
And my flesh is like the leaves.
I will be bare
Bones
Bleached white.
While I am still here,
I can feel joy,
I can feel love,
And most important,
I can feel your pain.
I can see your love sacrifices
You made for me,
And I can see others',
And that is what connects me with you.
I feel sympathy,
I care,
And when my emotions are full,
I cry.

So, while we're here,
Before our leaves are stripped from us,
Before we are bare on the earth,
Let us love.
Let us be in places
Where we can sympathize with each other,
Connected in love.
We live on.

By ourselves
We are bare branches,
Standing alone
Without the living spirit
Blowing between us.

# God's gift to me

My heart opens.
I feel all alone.
I feel like I don't want to go on.
I wish it were over.
And then I'll be in a group of people,
And someone will be talking,
And I will hear a witness
Of God's love in their life.
They don't call it God's love,
But what they did
Was loving,
Truly sacrificial,
Sacrificing himself for years
To protect another.
And when I hear
Of God's love and action,
I start to feel tears growing,
And I want to cry,
And all my feeling of being alone
Disappears.
I'm in a room
Where everyone is touched by love.
Even people who can't love
Are touched by those who do love,
And there are so many witnesses.
The room is full of them,
Because I can see their hearts opening.

I look around

And their eyes are open with love,

And we are together as one,

Witnesses of God's love in our lives.

We forget,

But God doesn't forget,

Because he brings his love to us

All day, through so many people,

In so many different ways,

And this is all we have to remember:

We live in a loving world,

And you do too.

# I know two women

When men
Say dumb things,
Because they're used to saying dumb things
And getting away with it,
Like it is their birthright
To just swagger through your life
And exist on swagger only,
Aired by a brutal spirit,
These two women
Cut them down,
Back them down,
And it takes a little while.
They are much smaller.
But they speak the truth.
And it has to
Be a concussion in the man
For him to finally get it.
And then, without saying "oh,"
They concede
The rightness of their words,
And these women stand up.
It would be hard for anybody
To speak their truth
In the face of such
Obtuse blindness,
But they bring the men back to reality.

They let them see
Where they are wrong,
And grudgingly the men
Cede territory.
And these women protect other women,
And they change
The space for the better,
And together
These two women
Make it safer for other women,
And they don't back down.

# I am glad

I am with the better part of the human race.
Yesterday it was just women,
And I thought how terrible it would be
To have to be among men only
For the rest of my life.
The women laughed
Naturally,
Motioning and gesturing,
Never like they would when men are present,
Because men are always watching,
And they would see them wiggling
And moving,
Their faces naturally beautiful.
It is sad they can't
Motion so quickly
And without restraint.
It is Man's eyes
Always looking at them
That keeps them
In this prison,
Because men act
On sight,
And their beauty unleashes them
To where they move
Forward.

I thought about these women,
Laughing
And relishing every word
Of other women,
And at the end of our meeting,
They were joined in beautiful conversations
All around the room
In groups of two,
Just laughing
And smiling.
I could never go back to the world of men.
They do not love each other this way.

# The voice I never expect

The voice I never
expect
Can stay silent for
seven years or forever.
And each time,
lying in the island,
With the tree blowing above me:
Thank You for the loon on the water.
Thank You for the still water.
Thank You for my back against the warm rock.
Thank You for the call across the water.
Thank You for the light in the morning.
Thank You. Thank You. Thank You.

www.ingramcontent.com/pod-product-compliance
Lightning Source LLC
LaVergne TN
LVHW081453060526
838201LV00050BA/1790